LIVING WELL
SAFETY ON THE
INTERNET

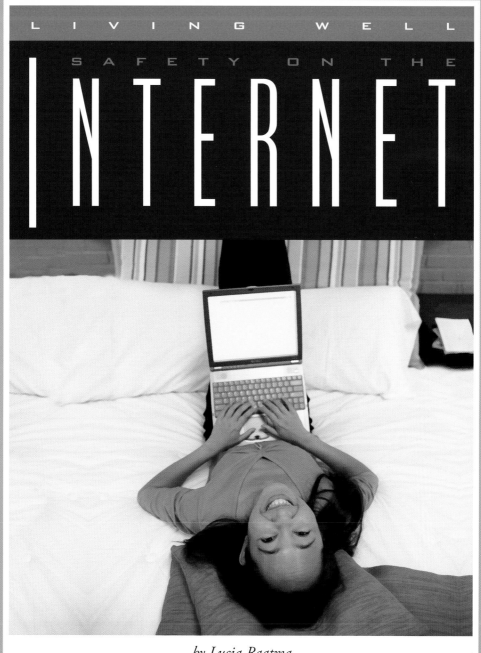

by Lucia Raatma

THE CHILD'S WORLD®
CHANHASSEN, MINNESOTA

Published in the United States of America by The Child's World®
PO Box 326, Chanhassen, MN 55317-0326
800-599-READ
www.childsworld.com

Subject Consultant:
Bridget Clementi,
Safe Kids Coordinator,
Children's Health
Education Center,
Milwaukee, Wisconsin

Photo Credits: Cover/frontispiece: Comstock/Punchstock; cover corner: Getty Images/Photodisc/Don Farrall. Interior: Corbis: 5 (LWA-JDC), 6, 7 (Bob Krist), 10, 14 (Roy McMahon), 17 (PictureNet), 19, 24 (William Whitehurst), 26 (Rick Gomez), 31 (James W. Porter); Tony Freeman/PhotoEdit: 13; Getty Images: 22 (Brand X Pictures/Randy Schwartz), 23 (The Image Bank/Inc. Gamma Ray Studio), 27 (Digital Vision); Getty Images/Photodisc: 8 (Don Farrall) 9 (Jason Reed/Ryan McVay); Getty Images/Photodisc/Daisuke Morita: 11, 20, 25; Jose Luis Pelaez Inc./Corbis: 15, 21; PictureQuest: 16 (Steve Cole/Photodisc), 18 (Stockbyte).

Editorial Directions, Inc.: E. Russell Primm, Editorial Director; Katie Marsico, Line Editor; Matt Messbarger, Editorial Assistant; Susan Hindman, Copy Editor; Sarah E. De Capua, Proofreader; Katherine Trickle and Stephen Carl Wender, Fact Checkers; Tim Griffin/IndexServ, Indexer; Cian Loughlin O'Day, Photo Researcher; Linda S. Koutris, Photo Selector

The Design Lab: Kathleen Petelinsek, Design; Kari Thornborough, Page Production

Library of Congress Cataloging-in-Publication Data
Raatma, Lucia.
   Safety on the Internet / By Lucia Raatma.
      v. cm. — (Living well (series))
   Includes bibliographical references and index.
   Contents: Daniel's school report—Safe surfing—E-mail, IMS, and netiquette—Knowing to whom you are talking—Guarding your computer—When it's time to sign off—Glossary—Questions and answers about Internet safety—Helping a friend learn about Internet safety— Did you know?—How to learn more about Internet safety.
   ISBN 1-59296-242-4 (Library bound : alk. paper)
   1. Internet and children—United States—Juvenile literature. 2. Internet—Security measures—United States—Juvenile literature. 3. Computer networks—Access control—United States—Juvenile literature. [1. Internet—Safety measures. 2. Safety.] I. Title. II. Living well (Child's World (Firm))
  HQ784.I58R33 2005
  025.04'028'9—dc22   2003027212

TABLE OF CONTENTS

CHAPTER ONE

DANIEL'S SCHOOL REPORT

It was Sunday night, and Daniel still needed to research a subject for one of his classes. He logged on to the Internet, typed "Gold Rush" into a **search engine,** and waited for a list of Web sites to appear. He found some great sites about both California and Alaska, and he read through the text. Then he saw one site with the message "For adults only—must be 18 to enter." Daniel exited the site and made a note of the Web address. He would tell his parents about that site later. It must have slipped through the **filter** they had put on the computer.

Just then an **instant message** (IM) notice appeared. "You have received an instant message from PatrickS. Do you wish to accept?" Daniel clicked yes. The message read: "Hey Dan. Did you see the game today?"

It was from his best friend, Patrick. He typed back: "Yeah, it was great. What a fourth quarter! Talk to you tomorrow, OK?" He liked chatting with Patrick, but he had to finish his homework.

A few minutes later, he got another notice. "You

The Internet is a good way to communicate with friends, but you still need to follow a few simple rules to stay safe.

have received an instant message from 432iluvyou. Do you wish to accept?" Daniel clicked no, and the notice disappeared. He did not know who that message was from.

After checking out a number of Web sites, Daniel felt ready to write his report. But before signing off, he decided to check his e-mail. There was one message from Tom, a member of his baseball team. Tom wondered if he could have a ride home from practice the next day. Daniel replied: "You bet. See you then."

There were two other e-mails. One was from a bookstore he liked to visit. The other one was from an address he did not recognize, and it had an **attachment.** Daniel deleted the message. Then he decided to log off. It was time to write that report.

When you check your e-mail, think twice before opening a message from a sender you don't recognize.

CHAPTER TWO

SAFE SURFING

Using the Internet is a great way to do research for school and to learn about new things. You can visit museums, explore national parks, and plan your next vacation. You can also shop on the Internet, where the stores are always open.

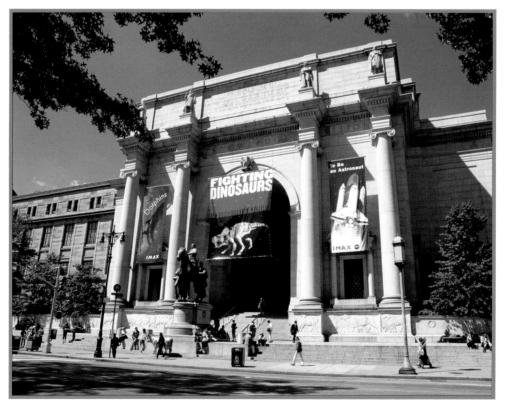

You may have always wanted to visit a museum in another state. Although it's fun to see exhibits in person, you can also explore your favorite attractions by surfing the Internet.

To keep all your travels on the Internet safe, you should follow a few rules. When surfing the Internet, steer clear of sites that are for adults only. If a site states that only those 18 and older can enter, take that warning seriously. Some material is not appropriate for kids. If you are unsure about a site, always ask a parent or another adult.

If you're preparing to enter a Web site and see a warning such as this one, visit another site instead.

If you want to shop on the Internet, always ask your parents' permission. They can help you fill out the shipping and payment information. Be sure you understand return **policies** and money-back **guarantees.** You don't

Online shopping can be exciting, but make sure you talk to an adult before purchasing or bidding on an item.

want to be stuck with something you don't like!

You can also shop on auction sites. The most popular of these is eBay, but there are many others. Again, have your parents help you if you want to purchase anything at such a site. Discuss with them how much you can spend on the item. They will help you with the bidding. Also understand the rules of bidding. Be sure not to offer a price that you really can't afford. After you make a bid, you may

not be able to cancel it if you change your mind later.

When visiting Web sites, be careful not to tell more about

yourself than you need to. For instance, if you are registering on

a site, don't give out your phone number or address unless it is

absolutely necessary. Check to see what information is required. Sometimes electronic ads called pop-up ads may appear on your screen. Don't click on these— you may be taken to a Web site that you did not intend to visit or that is for adults only.

Talk to your parents about what personal information you can safely share over the Internet. In most cases, it is better to tell as little about yourself as possible.

Choosing a Password

Be creative when you are choosing a password for your e-mail account or for sites that require registration. Don't select something that anyone can easily figure out. For instance, don't use your dog's name or your birthday. Instead, think of some-thing you—but no one else—can remember. Maybe your dad took you to your first baseball game when you were eight years old, and it was at Fenway Park. A good password might be dad8fen. This means a lot to you, but it is unlikely that someone else would think of it. It also uses a combination of numbers and letters, which makes it harder for other people to guess. Consider telling your parents your password in case you forget, but don't share this information with anyone else.

CHAPTER THREE

E-MAILS, IMs, AND NETIQUETTE

Sending and receiving e-mail is a fun way to communicate. You can also send IMs, which are as fast as talking on the phone! But it is important to follow a few rules.

With e-mail, pay attention to who gets copied when you send and receive a message. Sometimes, if you reply to an e-mail, you may end up replying to lots of people who received a copy of the original message. Be sure to check all the names you are responding to. Otherwise, you might send a message that other people shouldn't see. You could accidentally hurt someone's feelings or give away a secret.

When sending e-mail or IMs, it is also important to know the rules of **Netiquette.** Just as you should be polite and thoughtful to people you talk with on the phone or see in person,

you should also be courteous on the Internet. One rule is to

avoid using all capital letters, which can give the appearance that

you are shouting when you probably aren't. A more serious rule is

to never send threatening messages through the Internet. Even if

you are just kidding, such messages can get you in trouble. Your

Treat someone you meet on the Internet with the same respect and
courtesy you would show that person if you met him face to face.

It's best not to send e-mail if you're angry at someone. Whether you're on the playground or in front of your computer, it's always a good idea to cool off before you respond to someone you're mad at.

Internet service provider (ISP) may discontinue your service. Or you could even be arrested. So be careful what you write. And if you are angry at someone, take some time to cool off before you respond to that person.

If you ever receive a threatening message from someone, talk to an adult right away. An adult can help you decide how serious the matter is. You may want to report the person to their ISP, or you may need to contact the police. Or you may simply choose to avoid communicating with that person in the future.

Receiving a threatening message from someone can be frightening. Speaking to a trusted adult as soon as possible will make you feel better and will help you decide how to handle the situation.

CHAPTER FOUR

KNOW WHO'S ONLINE

Sometimes it is fun to be **anonymous** on the Internet. You can use a mysterious name in a **chat room,** and no one will know who you are. But remember, other people may do the same thing. So a person claiming to be a 13-year-old girl who loves shopping may really be someone else.

You might not recognize someone if he is wearing a mask. Guests in chat rooms can also hide their true identities, so be careful when chatting with someone you do not know.

Keep in mind that chat room guests can lie about their age, location, and identity. Someone who is 60 could say he is 15, and it is almost impossible to know if that person is telling the truth.

"She" could be a college student having a little fun—or worse, an older man or woman who is trying to meet young boys or girls.

Never give out your full name, address, phone number, or school name when you are chatting with people you don't know. And do not e-mail a photo of yourself to anyone you do not

You might become good friends with someone on the Internet, but your mom or dad may want to go with you if you plan on meeting her in person.

know. If someone asks to meet you in person, talk to your parents right away. They may feel that if they accompany you and the meeting is in a public place, it is OK. Or they may decide it is a bad idea. Listen to your parents, and never meet anyone without their permission.

It is sad—and a little scary—to realize that

some people on the Internet are trying to trick you. Every year, hundreds of kids are kidnapped, and some of them were **lured** by people on the Internet. So have fun chatting, but be careful.

If you are suspicious or uncomfortable about anyone on the Internet, tell your parents right away. And if you get IMs from someone you do not know, do not answer them.

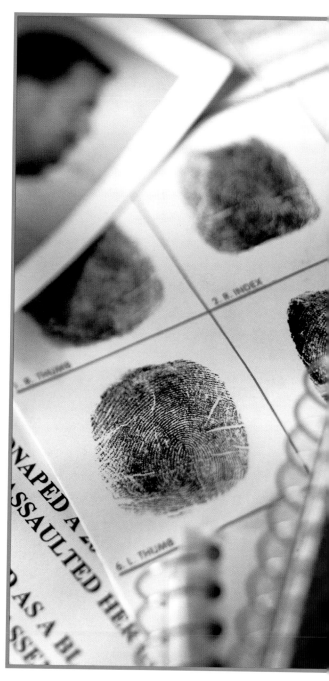

Many of the people you meet on the Internet are probably nice, but some may be kidnappers. This is why it is always important to be cautious when chatting with strangers.

Talk to your parents about the rules for Internet use. This list is a good start:

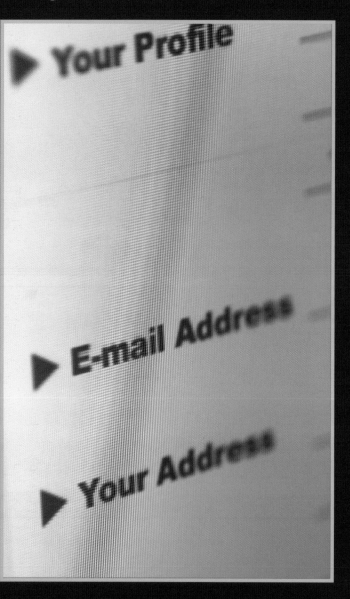

1. Never give your Internet password to anyone, except your parents.

2. Never open e-mail attachments from someone you do not know.

3. Never e-mail a photo of yourself to someone you do not know, unless your parents say it is OK.

4. Never give out your full name, address, phone number, or school name to someone you do not know.

5. Always tell your parents if you come across a Web site that is for adults only.

6. Always tell your parents if someone on the Internet threatens you or makes you feel uncomfortable.

7. Always be courteous with   **your home such as the living**

CHAPTER FIVE

GUARDING YOUR COMPUTER

Have you ever stayed home because you had a virus? Well, computers can get viruses, too, and they can get really sick. A **computer virus** can damage your computer or possibly even destroy your hard drive. Most viruses are sent through e-mail attachments. Some-times a person will accidentally send a document with a virus in it. Other

Just as you miss school school because of the flu, a computer is not able to work properly if it is infected by a virus.

*Some people intentionally send out computer viruses, so it is always wise
to think twice before opening e-mail from someone you don't know.*

times, however, people send viruses on purpose. Never open an

attachment that is sent by someone you do not know. It is best to

just delete the e-mail altogether. Some e-mails with addresses you

You can install software on your computer that will help protect it from viruses. In some cases, you can even download programs from the Internet that will reduce the amount of spam you receive through e-mail.

do not recognize may only be **spam.** But deleting these e-mails

is still a good idea.

It is a good idea to have virus protection software on your

computer. Talk to your parents about adding it if you do not have it already. These software programs run scans of your hard drive every week or every month. They also check any document that you are downloading.

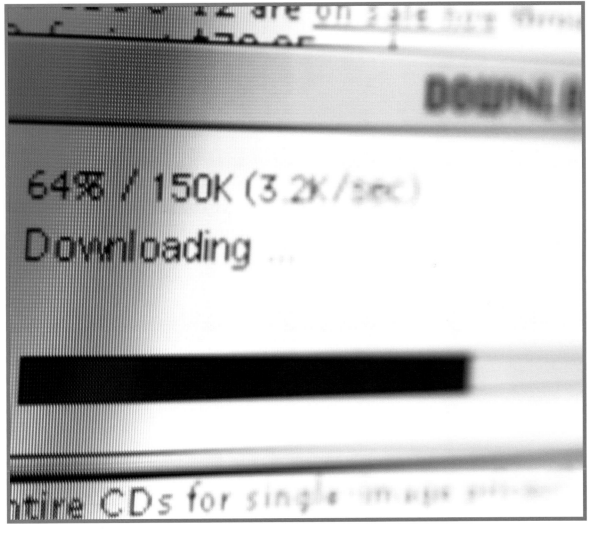

Sometimes people accidentally download documents that contain computer viruses, but protective software prevents this from happening by detecting a virus early on.

CHAPTER SIX

WHEN IT'S TIME
TO SIGN OFF

Time may seem to fly by when you are on the Internet. Chatting

with friends or playing games can be lots of fun. But know when

it is time to sign off. Seeing your friends in person, spending time

with your family, and keeping up with

schoolwork are all important.

So make sure you

are not ignoring

other parts of your

life because of

the Internet.

Talk to your

parents about

Surfing the Internet is fun, but you should always leave time to do your homework and be with the people you care about.

guidelines for Internet use. Decide on time limits and discuss the

dangers you might face on the Internet. The more you know, the

safer you will be.

*Talk to your parents about the Internet. They can help
you with any questions or concerns you may have.*

Glossary

anonymous (uh-NON-uh-muhss) Remaining anonymous means keeping your name or identity unknown.

attachment (uh-TACH-muhnt) An attachment is a document or image that is sent with an e-mail.

chat room (CHAT ROOM) A chat room is a site where people can send messages as quickly as they could talk in person or on the phone.

computer virus (kuhm-PYOO-tur VYE-russ) A computer virus is a software program, often sent in e-mail attachments, that is designed to harm computers.

filter (FIL-tur) A filter is a software program that separates Web sites that you have access to from those that you don't.

guarantees (ga-ruhn-TEEZ) Guarantees are promises made by manufacturers that they will repair or replace a product you bought from them if it breaks or doesn't work. Most guarantees require that you tell manufacturers about such problems within a certain period of time after buying the product.

instant message (IN-stuhnt MESS-ij) An instant message is a note sent on the Internet and is abbreviated IM.

Internet service provider (in-TUR-net SUR-viss pruh-VIDE-ur) An Internet service provider is a company that gives people access to the Internet and is abbreviated ISP.

lured (LOORD) A person who is lured is led into danger by someone or something that looks attractive.

Netiquette (NET-uh-ket) Netiquette is a system of manners and rules for the Internet.

policies (POL-uh-seez) Policies are insurance plans that people are encouraged to read when they purchase a product.

search engine (surch EN-juhn) A search engine is an Internet tool that finds related sites based on keywords that you provide.

spam (spam) Spam is junk mail that is sent as e-mail.

Questions and Answers about Internet Safety

If I am not using my real name on the Internet, I can say whatever I want, right? Not necessarily. Even if you are anonymous, you should be careful about what you say. You do not want to hurt anyone's feelings. And you should not say anything threatening. Such messages can be traced by ISPs or the police.

Someone in a chat room seems really nice. She wants to meet me at the mall. Is that OK? Talk to your parents right away! If this person is really a nice girl your age, meeting her may be OK—as long as someone goes with you and your parents agree. But this person may really be someone trying to trick you.

I keep getting e-mail from a person I do not know. What should I do? Delete the e-mails. But if they keep coming, contact your ISP.

My friends like to IM for hours and hours. But I get tired of it. What should I say? Tell your friends that you love chatting with them, but you can only stay on the Internet for a set amount of time. Remind them how fun it is to get together in person.

Helping a Friend Learn about Internet Safety

▸ Practice sending e-mails and IMs with your friends. Give each other advice about Netiquette issues.

▸ Show your friend the virus protection service you have. Together, watch the program scan your documents for viruses.

▸ Review the rules for staying safe online (on pages 20–21) with your friend. You both can talk about why each rule is important.

Did You Know?

▸ About 45 million children and teens have Internet access.

▸ The Internet did not come into general use until around 1995. It had not been invented when your parents were growing up.

▸ You shouldn't believe everything you read online! Some sites have faulty information.

How to Learn More about Internet Safety

At the Library
Gralla, Preston. *Online Kids: A Young Surfer's Guide to Cyberspace.*
New York: Wiley, 1999.

Rothman, Kevin F. *Coping with Dangers on the Internet: A Teen's Guide to
Staying Safe Online.* New York: Rosen, 2000.

Sherman, Josepha. *Internet Safety.* Danbury, Conn.: Franklin Watts, 2003.

On the Web
Visit our home page for lots of links about Internet safety:
http://www.childsworld.com/links.html

Note to Parents, Teachers, and Librarians: We routinely verify our
Web links to make sure they're safe, active sites—so encourage your
readers to check them out!

Through the Mail or by Phone
Federal Bureau of Investigation
Crimes against Children Program
935 Pennsylvania Avenue NW
Room 11163
Washington, DC 20535
202/324-3666

National SAFE KIDS Campaign
1301 Pennsylvania Avenue NW
Suite 100
Washington, DC 20004
202/662-0600

Index

About the Author

Lucia Raatma received her bachelor's degree in English literature from the University of South Carolina and her master's degree in cinema studies from New York University. She has written a wide range of books for young people. When she is not researching or writing, she enjoys going to movies, practicing yoga, and spending time with her family. She lives in New York.